The Forest That Knows

101 Songs and Poems about Nature, Including
Water, Trees, Animals, Birds, the Sun,
Seasons and Weather

Books by Matt Kavan

Flopping on the Deck
The Forest That Knows
Thirsty Dreams
Here For a Moment
Here's To
The Morning Catch

The Forest That Knows

101 Songs and Poems about Nature, Including
Water, Trees, Animals, Birds, the Sun,
Seasons and Weather

Matt Kavan

Matt Kavan
2014

Copyright © 2014 by Matt Kavan

First Printing: 2014

ISBN: 978-1-312-36866-8

Matt Kavan
www.mattkavan.com

Book Cover Graphics: The painting River Valley was created by Paul Kavan.

Ordering Information:
Special discounts are available on quantity purchases by corporations, associations, educators, and others. For details, contact the publisher at the above listed address.

Dedication

To nature, full of creatures evolving features for adapting
scenes and laughing in trees.

Contents

Introduction

While being in nature can generally be seen as a relaxing getaway, which it often is, when looking closely there's always something going on. In the water fish are regularly attacking and eating each other, on land animals are busily staking out their territories, and the air is filled with flocks, vultures, and trillions of mosquitoes or other bugs constantly in search of a new trough. Yet it's alive and not always at each others throats, occasionally the waters are calm, it's a nice day out, trees are everywhere, and various animals or birds will stop by to check you out, curiosity looking itself in the mirror.

In The Forest That Knows are seven sections, the first being Nature, with ones that are often about more than a single area, such as in the water, land or air with fish, animals or birds, and usually a combination. After the general overview is water, where much of life begins and includes oceans, lakes and rivers along with activities one can do, such as fishing. From the water you have the earth and trees, including mountains, bridges, forests and various types of trees. With the land are the living creatures or animals such as snakes, ants, deer, lions and anything else that crawls or runs. Moving skyward are the birds, including blue jays, owls and ravens. Continuing skyward is the sun and its never-ending ripple effects and finally ending with seasons and the weather, putting everything we know in flux, yet with a pattern as regular as the seasons.

One of the problems with writing about nature is that once you're in it, and probably in the best position to capture it, you really don't want to be writing and prefer to be involved, even if that simply means paying attention. Whether it be spotting a pelican diving for a fish, a turtle popping its head up to check you out, a battle between two birds in flight, or just watching some bug

1

move slowly across your path, either way, you notice they're in their own worlds, doing their own thing and mostly oblivious to your presence. Or occasionally annoyed of you getting too close to their turf, unless of course you have bread or food to offer, then you're their best friend and paying attention to your every move.

Of all the fish, animals and birds out there, one of the more interesting ones are ravens. When it's windy they'll be diving and twisting in the wind, doing tricks and getting kicks with flying straight towards the ground and spinning in circles about 30 times before correcting themselves and back up to do it again. For food, while known for making raids, stealing and stashing, nobody can doubt their creativity while doing so. They can even be impromptu musicians, having seen them join in on a tune and keeping in step, cawing at the end of every line. Then there's the stories and mythologies, going back from ancient times through today, always on the edges of events, leading the way or picking up the scraps left over.

That said, most creatures get interesting the more you know about them, usually being difficult as they're never keeping still, offering only an occasional glimpse to outsiders. Except of course trees, fascinating in their own right but not as interactive. The Forest That Knows is a collection of songs or poems that touch on these aspects, as well as some of the meanings, symbolism, or perspectives one can find from them.

Nature

A Natural Escape

Getting away, from the traffic and cities
Feeling to stray, towards mountains and valleys
Maybe an ocean, a lake or a river
Never knowing the ending until later
What you'll see, what happens next
Into a world and leaving a crutch
From modern scenes and technologies
Following paths surrounded by trees
Hearing the birds, the squirrels give a warning
Seeing a glimpse, never full showing
All types of species, together and alone
Searching for food or building a home
Maybe to play, enjoying the day
Meeting a human in a curious way
Building a fire, watching the stars
Asking some questions of who we are
Echoes from owls, hearing some howls
Wake in the rain, smelling the flowers
Heading on back, from a long overdue break
Returning from roots, a natural escape

Acquaintances

The black cat and the raven
Occasionally will cross paths
Used to be with the dolphin
Before the choices were cast

Actions

Fly like an eagle
Swim like a shark
Sleep like a bear
Dig like an aardvark

Jump like a dolphin
Run like a cheetah
Dive like a pelican
Think like a fox

Joke like a raven
Walk like a cat
Drink like a camel
Hear like a bat

Where we're from
Where we go
That we do it
All to know

Don't Be Surprised

If you really must
Try and try again
Don't be surprised
Of the tragic end
For the snake that bites
The shark that feasts
It's in their nature
Tread carefully

Glimpses

Hear the wolf in the night
Howling for a home
A dog feels a tear
A lost, forgotten home

Along comes the wily cat
Somewhere in between
Other worlds, there and back
Follow edges of a scene

See the bird fly in from above
A bluebird or a hawk
Where it comes or goes I'll never know
To join or leave the flock

Growing

Growing older
The wind gets colder

Growing younger
Feel the hunger

Growing up
Fill up the cup

Growing down
Roots to sound

Growing left
Seek a theft

Growing right
Laughing delight

Home

The bird finds its nest
The river finds its sea
The salmon finds its rest
The human finds a tree
A quest or a jest
With others or alone
Forever we search
Traces of home

Living Today

See the diamonds on the water, the early morning dew
All the greens in the trees, ocean and sky are blue
A desert of sand to the beach on the shore
The mountains to climb, showing a whole lot more
Just a few things you'll see in the day
No longer a dream, living today

See the rising of the sun, the fullness of the moon
The rooster waking up, the early bird gets the worm
The deer runs in fields, an eagle flying high
An otter on the surface, pelicans for the dive
Just a few things you'll see in the day
No longer a dream, living today

See a train leaving town, a flashing green light
A walk in the park with the sun shining bright
A ship heading out to a foreign horizon
A plane flying by into the sun setting
Just a few things you'll see in the day
No longer a dream, living today

Find new friends to greet, experiences to share
New creations discovered, a book to compare
New music seeping in, favorite places to visit
Returning again, a home to rest in
Just a few things you'll see in the day
No longer a dream, living today

Nature

If one likes nature so much
Try inviting mosquitoes for lunch
Maybe a grizzly or a hungry snake
Swim with a shark and a bloody scrape
Survival of the fittest, defines its game
With the only purpose, more of the same
Adapting and tweaking, to the outer world
Space and time, seasons are hurled
In such a world, security is key
Thieves are all, seeking energy
Living on taking, the same old story
Until creating, a different glory
Nothing tragic, it's just its nature
But where does the comic, fit in the picture

Only the Dream

Sitting on the shore, searching the sea for more
No boat with an oar, only dreams to explore
Where they go, never taking long
With waves are crashing, ending the song

Back to the world, busy as bees
Nature has led, extending through trees
Follow the seasons and stories of old
Into the spring, awaken to grow

Getting time to go, the sun has almost set
Back to the path, traveled by cats
Finding a cave, in the side of a hill
Building a fire, escaping the chill

Seeing the stars, scattering the sky
Shapes and dimensions, a question of why
Watching the logs, burning to ash
Only the dream, was ever meant to last

Outside the Window

The birds outside are chirping
The fox on the side is lurking
The hawk is silent above it all
The raven laughs at every fall

Sea to Sky

Take me to the sea
Where so many are swimming free
From the shallows to the depths
A little bit of ancient inside of me

But I can never return
The path is left to burn
Float in the warm, sunny breeze
Pages remain to unlearn

Take me to the sky
Where the stars will never deny
Climbing ladders, mirrors are shattered
With the dream and boat to fly

The Darkened Sphere

The darkened sphere
Is full of fear
See the signs
Ain't it clear
Covering up
The past is done
Confuse with lies
Hide the sun

Wake From the Fog

Through the mist and fog laying thickly
On a path in the woods moving quickly
Hear the owls ring the bells perceiving
See the ravens show the way conceiving
To the edge of a mountain clearing
The clouds far below are showing
The heights that you've gone in the dark
Never knowing how long or far
Feeling at the end of a road
A bridge you see for a hope
It's old and thin, can't see where it ends
Turn around, hear a growl that sends
You forward above the depths far below
The steps adding up for hours you go
For days or more hard to tell anymore
Feel the wind begin to swing the floor
Lose the grip falling faster through the wind
Wondering how far it goes to the end
After awhile you smile with a trick
The Lotus for riding a magic carpet
Where to go next always hard to say
Waking up for the start of another day

Walking Days

How many miles did I walk today
In the sun or down in hades
Sometimes faster or grinding to a halt
Being chased or fall down flat

In between I'll check out the scene
Up a mountain or down a stream
Either way, never staying around too long
Traps are set if you don't belong

I wish it were different but I am aware
Of all the games that a group will dare
No worries, no bother, I won't offend
Only these moments before the end

Water

A Day at the Lake

Hear the loon sing a tune
Even owls like it too
In the dawn, dusk and noon
Always singing, aren't we cool

See the beaver building
A new home in the bay
All the sticks are mixing
Hiding doors from the stray

Bringing fish that it's found
Splashing water for a warning
Chewing trees from the ground
Always busy doing something

So many seagulls
On the lake or the shore
Looking out for scraps
From the fish caught before

Pelicans with a purpose
Diving from sky to water
Coming up with a grin
Single bites clean the platter

The golden one is the fish
That most will try to catch
Some will be too big
And end up going back

Hanging out in the deep
The burbot chills all day
The only type of cod
To ever find in a lake

Some people like them
Others not so much
Mostly depending
Who's cleaning for lunch

The largest crappies you'll ever see
Can be found in the spring
Otherwise you might as well
Find another song to sing

In the shallow or the deep
Perch are everywhere
A tasty treat for all to feed
In the water or the air

Caw, caw, caw says the crow
Of a feast it has found
Or an answer to a joke
And the laughing is the sound

Soaring high and far
The Bald Eagle can be seen
Grabbing fish on the fly
Nesting in the tallest tree

The vultures will be granted
To eat what others won't
As long as it's not planted
Could be found on the road

Deer on sides of highways
Or meadows in the evening
Maybe across the lake
Will sometimes be swimming

When camping in the woods
A bigger home you're in
All will smell your goods
With the bears calling dibs

In the spring you'll see
Turtles digging holes
For the rest in the sea
See the new borns, go, go, go

Millions of tiny minnows
Swimming around the lake
From the reefs in the deep
To the weeds in the bay

So many different ducks
With a quack you will know
Some ducklings on a trip
In the bay that they know

Tiny little helicopters
Flying along the shore
Heading for a feast
Of mosquitoes galore

With a certain smell you will know
That a skunk has just passed
Black and whites stripes will show
Searching for others scraps

When the sun goes down
The frogs are awake
Singing their song
Croaking all the way

Another day at the lake
Never knowing what will be
Until the splash or the wake
Living in the mystery

A Refuge

Sitting by the water
Hear the ripples on the shore
It couldn't get much better
Days ahead or long before
Watching the seagulls fly
Hear the calling of the loon
A refuge or place to hide
From distractions calling soon

Bay of Dreams

It's all been done and said before
Being different a harder chore
Have to go deeper or some other way
Find the river from a forgotten bay
Holding the dreams, the way to go forward
Before the source is completely covered
By so many distractions and games
Scents and sounds blocking the way

Have to listen deeper for the ancient beat
Looking clearer where strangers meet
Taste the fruit from the knowing stream
Smell the flowers that call the bees
Touch the land from blue to green
Find the way to the bay of dreams
Not so easy I'd think you'd agree
All sorts of traps and false tributaries

Detours aplenty that you only learn later
The refuge was made for you on a platter
Rarely getting caught up with the rubes
Staying back from shows to amuse
Lucky a few times when pushing too far
Break a few lines with hooks in the jaw
After awhile the scene starts to change
Seeing a school and rules of the same

So far to go and no time to waste
Mostly uphill the refuge will take
Have a few jokes for the struggle of the day
Mostly different unexpected delays
Just when you think everything is fine
Find a waterfall of an impossible climb
Must be a detour how can this be
The source so strong cannot disagree

Even worse there's teeth at the top
Open are bared and ready to snap

Circling back and finding others in wait
Carcasses scattered in realms of decay
Going faster than ever been done before
Leaping higher and over the roar
Landing down with a splash in the water
Into the bay of dreams thereafter

Boat or Blue

Who am I
Who are you
In the boat
Out is blue

Boats

So many tribes
Groups and cultures
Riding their boats
Guarding their treasure

Anything different
Always the same
Mostly a weight
Rarely a claim

Slow and steady
Nobody rocks the boat
Too many times
Water overflow

Where are they going
What is their purpose
Lost over time
Too many detours

Connecting again
On the unknown horizon
Follow the trend
With wind to rely on

Bring the Boat to the Shore

Bring the boat to the shore
From the sky or across the sea
Been waiting so long, I fell on the floor
Maybe one too many or three
A little banged up and sore
From all the quests I couldn't ignore
Followed the fool but never got free
Bring the boat to the shore

Dawn on the Lake

In the morning, after a storm
The sun is rising, starting to warm
The sky is clear, the water is blue
A gentle breeze, birds chirping too
Looking at the lake, see a thousand sparkles
Dancing on the waves, a bridge ever widening
A cup of coffee, waking up with the day
All is anew, a dawn on the lake

Fishing

Catch a fish
Make a wish
Where it goes
Nobody knows

Floating

Floating in a whirlpool
Spinning round and round
Stretching out for miles
On the edges are the towns

Over days, months and years
Inching ever closer to the core
Paddle as fast as you want
Escaping is the shore

Falling to the middle
Over time or a sudden stop
Dropping to the depths
To the city full of crocs

Through sparkles of diamonds
Twisting ribbons of silk
All your questions answered
Drawing closer still

Except for the one of course
Stopping illusions grand
Where to find the tree
That needs no type of land

The earth starts to quake
The fire surges high
The waters leave to part
Floating to the sky

From Sea to Sky

The chaos of the water
Getting heavy with the weight
Good luck swimming through it
Good luck being saved

Rising to the surface
Feel the sun cover all
Seeing birds flying higher
No fear of the fall

Walk on two legs or four
Slither across the land
Stuck on the ground
Castles in the sand

With waves washing over
Inevitable fate
Hopping on a boat
From the sky to escape

Hope You Can Float

Burn up the oil
Burn up the coal
Melt everything
And hope you can float

Into the Mist

Bursting through
The abyss of dreary
Drops of dew
When feeling weary
Is it possible
Or an imagined dream
How much struggle
Is needed to see
Past the surface
An ocean in wait
No more objects
Words to say
Diving deeper
To the city below
Escape the reaper
The traps to know
Anything new
Or the same old tricks
Rising again
Into the mist

Lady of the Water

Dragging a bag of bones across the street
Past the empty houses and nobody to meet
Through the graveyard and a barren wood
Down to the lake where the lady stood
Through the air the bag is thrown
Flying fair in the arms a home
Those bones aren't for me, who knows where I found them
Back to the sea, a note was surrounding
Not wanting to anger, bring on a curse from the dead
Too many already, swimming in my head
A smile was replied with a nod for the trouble
This won't be forgotten we're all in a struggle
When the time comes and you've met your end
Bring your bones to me and I'll make amends
So from that day forward everywhere I go
Never touched the land, on a boat did float
Played band on a cruise, an extra hand on a charter
Hijacked by pirates, left to drift on much farther
Landing on an island after a few steps I collapse
With the rising tide in the ocean I'm swept
Into the water with my bones no matter
Into the arms of the lady in the water

Lake Afternoons

Quietly sitting
On a shore of a lake
A gentle breeze blowing
The mosquitoes away

With a line in the water
Some coffee or drink
Removing all the clutter
Giving room to think

Watching ripples rolling by
A turtle or a loon
The clouds in the sky
Simply living afternoons

Salmon in the Stream

Adapt to the dream
The ever winding flow
Salmon in the stream
Showing all there is to know

Scenic Surroundings

When fishing and catching
Not a thing at all
Could be worse, you're not working
The clocks and cubes to fall
All the scenic surroundings
Where the creatures do belong
See the leaves gently blowing
With the waves, make the song

Sharks

Swimming in the depths
For thousands of years
Little has changed
Always are feared

The lion of the sea
Hundreds of teeth to bare
Devour everything
Little can compare

Stories have been told
Movies have been made
No boat is too big
For a shark, you're the bait

People come and go
Civilizations rise and fall
Other species evolve
The shark has seen it all

Sitting on the Shore

With the full moon shining
An evening has begun
Here the lone wolf howling
Calling to the sun
With a warm breeze bristling
The leaves from the trees
The branches are dancing
With shadows to please

Chorus
Just another evening
Sitting on the shore
Stay for a while
Open some doors

An owl sneaking in
An end is coming soon
Movements from the lake
A loon sings a tune
The frogs have a chat
Some fish are on the move
See the flying bats
Across the brightened moon

Chorus

See a shooting star
Across the milky way
A turtle searching for
A safer place to lay
Feel the warmth from the fire
Reaching to the sky
All the songs and stories
Laughing no deny

Chorus

Struggle for Laughter

Catching a fish
Is all good and fun
So are the times
When nothing is done
For in the end
It doesn't really matter
Moments to spend
Struggle for laughter

The Lotus

Throw me all your tricks
To see if I pass the test
On the water is the Lotus
Flying higher while at rest

The Shore Fisherman

He sits alone, fishing on the shore
Watching all the boats go by
They're heading off to, a far away place
Finding where the fish do hide
If only they knew, what he's been through
And why he seems content and fine
Catching some beers, losing the fears
Throwing out a hookless line

Taking out a flute and letting it loose
Getting a beat from the waves
Feeling the sun, wind in the trees
Starting a song to wake
The crow is the first, the seagulls are next
Pelicans and eagles too
From the land, the squirrels and the fox
Beavers and turtles in blue

As the hours roll by, the fish can't deny
Swimming closer to the tune
The minnows are first, feeling the thirst
Others think they're hearing loons
All the big fish move in, as fast as can swim
The bay is getting all filled up
With all joined in, sing if they can
Or dancing with a fin in step

The setting of the sun, the music to end
Everyone takes their leave
The boats return, red from the burn
Of a fruitless day on the sea
Not sure what went wrong, not a nibble was found
How did you do by the way
With a broken line, played this flute of mine
Ending up being all day

Water Drops

Where the river starts, a shallow lake
Beginning as a gentle stream
After awhile, others pass the way
The river is picking up steam
Getting deeper and wider, hearing the thunder
An upcoming waterfall
Crashing down soon, into a pool
The highest you ever saw

Keep going again, around a bend
From mountains to the valley below
If you listen closely, you can hear the band
Humming to the songs that flow
No words to speak, no signs of the weak
A flowing and surging sound
Through calm and storms, bright or bleak
Winding past the cities and towns

Arriving at last, an ocean so vast
After having been gone so long
Hearing the beats, waves give a crash
Another banging of the gong
Collecting again, with so many friends
Every drop is to their own
Settling in, no asking of when
Arriving at a home

After some years, seeing the sun
Rising into the mist
Blowing away, clouds on the run
Heading where the lands do thirst
With a spark and a boom, over too soon
Landing with little plop
Next thing you know, hearing the loon
The life of a water drop

Waves Crashing

What is the value
Of hearing waves crashing
Blasting away
All your distractions

Land and Trees

Above and Below

What's above or
What's below
Eat the fruit
With roots to know

Becoming a Tree

Walking through a forest, with trees all around
Some higher than others, directions are found
Climb to the top, scanning the scene
Where else to go, follow the dream

Finding a mountain, up through the clouds
Cliffs and gorges, walling the ground
Get to the peak, can see everything
What else is left, defining is bleak

Start down again, a weekend to mend
Conquer the world, to balance within
Back to the path, with rails holding back
Into the box, cheese in the trap

Or so was the plan, but something went wrong
Could no longer return, repetitive song
Stuck at the edge, with trees for a hedge
Banging a drum, raising the dead

Of so many ancient, legends and myths
Mixing together, follow the roots
Going much deeper, than our feet can know
Where it ends, planting to grow

Dig in your heels, making a stand
Feeling the ground, wiggle the land
Arms moving out, stretching for fun
Out comes the leaves, capture the sun

Growing so tall, circle the earth
Roots to surround, feeling the worth
To the stars above, and farther I feel
Until the fall, that much is clear

Bottom of Roots

What is the answer
What is the truth
Will be found
At the bottom of roots

Bridge Problems

Temptations abound
Welcome to the bridge
Good luck to pass
Wide as the edge
Or so it seems
With pride so full
Small as the flea
Few worries to mull
Or riddles there are
Perspectives to show
The near and the far
The clocks are all broke
Just the way it goes
When crossing the bridge
Passing by the trolls
Hopping to the ledge

Climbing Trees

Finding a tree, it's so very tall
Start at the bottom, nowhere to fall
Grabbing a branch, beginning with one
What could it hurt, closer to sun

After many more, getting high off the ground
One after another, knowledge is found
Learning everything, every branch and leaf
After awhile, a joker or thief

Getting to the top, for the cherished fruit
Feeling the beat, with no more blues
What's after that, take a look around
A much higher tree, the top isn't found

How to move over, a jump or a leap
Falling so fast, building up speed
Turn on your brain, is this your fate
Start slowing down, feel to create

Taller and higher, there is no end
Trying to make, an upward trend
For as long as you can, can barely stand
Planting new roots, in so many lands

Earth and Sky

The earth and sky
A struggle to balance
Walking the line
An inward reliance

Follow the Sound

Stuck in a land
Drawn to the ground
How to escape
Follow the sound

Hearing the Band

Visiting a land
That few have known
Hearing the band
From the tree that grows

Leaving to Shade

When nothing works out as planned
Welcome to reality, a foreign land
Stepping out of your shell, away from the board
So many others, travel their worlds

Sooner or later, you'll surely figure out
Easier said than done, no bother to shout
No more talking, no more delay
Capture the moments that make up the day

One at a time, who cares how small or big
Climbing the vine, so much more there is
Falling again, from another random breeze
No roots to hold when getting bleak

This isn't right, there has to be another way
Planting your own, with the sun and rain
Slowly at first, fragile to break
Branches of perspectives, with fruit to take

Years rolling by, reaching towards the sky
Taller than mountains, no clouds will deny
With roots stretching out, circling the earth
Feeling the vibe, what is it worth

Others have tried, to bring it down hard
Axes and bombs, are left in chards
With bark a matter, stronger than all
The winds will gather, when hearing the call

How long does it last, what happens next
The birds will show, leaving the nest
Until then, nothing to do but grow
Leaving to shade, the trees that know

Never Meant to Last

Born on a branch of the tree
How high I was never told
Reaching to the end to touch the leaves
Slipping off and down I go

It doesn't take long until hitting a branch
Getting wider the farther down
Landing to stop where I can stand
Still not quite on the ground

Climbing again, going up and straight
No longer entertaining detours
Get to the top, such a lonely place
Too high for the streams and flowers

What to do next, feel the winds of change
A house of cards falling fast
Landing on the ground, feeling strange
Never meant to last

Perspectives

What do you see
What do you know
The falling leaves
Or roots to grow

Roads to Bridges

When roads turn to bridges
You never know what might happen
Traveling over air
Where the birds will gather

Rocks and Trees

Rocks are old and wise
Staying put for time to fly
From the bottom of the sea to the sky
They've seen it all and know why

Trees are tall and free
With roots holding steady to be
Seasons change through the centuries
Sun and rain grows the seed

Life is full of highs and lows
Maybe with others or alone
In the wind or cast in stone
Moving through, find a home

Roots and Leaves

Planting a seed
Growing a tree
Digging with roots
Shedding with leaves

Start Up the Trail

Hunting for lions
Fishing for whales
Look at the eagle
Start up the trail

The Crooked Tree

In the land of the trees, there was one that stood out
It never went straight, twisting branches throughout
It's slower than most, can never quite keep up
The race to the sun, the winners with trump

Dodging this way and that, find bits and pieces
The end was so tangled, a struggle no sleeping
Seemed doomed to the end, only a matter of time
Without any sun, too slow for the climb

Along came one day, an axe man looking for pay
Seeing the forest, his ship has been saved
Debt to the hilt, this will take care of everything
So many so straight, the highest to bring

After awhile, the land was left bare
With only one left, the man would declare
This ones so crooked, it's not worth my time
I'll cash in my chips, buy barrels of wine

All left alone, a crooked tree on a hill
Surrounded by stumps, their pride cut to nill
Just the way it goes, in the modern world
Anything too straight, end in the mill

The Forest That Knows

The shadows that grow from the forest that knows
Stretch to the ends where the water flows
The creatures that hide from the reapers glance
The features that provide attractions to dance
Where in the green do the roots have dreams
Without being trimmed and left is free
It starts in the middle answering the riddle
On your own outside of the bubble
Outside of the books, the leaves of the day
Starting with seeds, spring no delay

Trees to Sky

Walking through the wind and rain
Leaves and trees know the way
Secrets known will not say
Keys through doors, no random stray
All the same at the end of the day
Except the one in your brain

Where it goes nobody knows
Sometimes fast, others slow
See the dots, tendencies show
Getting higher or down it flows
Feel the rain, help it grow
Preparing for the forgotten boat

Floating down from the sky
A bottled message, in your mind
Opened up for a rhyme
Adding music, killing time
What it means, all in signs
See the fool, deaf and blind

Walking Through the Forest

Walking through the forest
So many types of trees
The ancients above the rest
New ones in the weeds

Some have fruit to bare
Others become a home
Some are green all the year
Others not in snow

In the end from ax or storm
Falling to the ground
To the earth losing form
Or a fire higher bound

For my own roots and branches
Not so high but more than some
Ideas the fruit set to blossom
From the rain and the sun

Where it goes, lots of hybrids
Floating in the wind
Landing on a foreign island
Another forest to begin

Animals

A Beaten Wolf

The wolf has been beaten
It's lying on the floor
On a leash but no weeping
Of ancient strands before
Just passing the time
Will it ever end
An occasional howl
When the moon cannot bend

A Houyhnhnm to Know

The flocks and the herds collectively learn
The squirrels climbing trees with nuts to earn
The snake lies in wait for a victim to pass
The lion takes a toll from a chosen cast
The eagle sees it all from a higher perspective
The dragons had the fall from too many reflections
The salmon with the struggle finding their way home
The horse running free a Houyhnhnm to know

Animal World

Ants you see marching, by the scent they will know
Bluebirds give a squawk, for a trough that will grow
Crocodiles grinning, from their meal on the take
Deer will be running, for a safer field to play
Eagles flying higher, with telescopic eyes
Foxes hiding out, always on the sly
Giraffes standing tall, sleeping minutes a day
Hippos staying cool, in the water or shade

Chorus
All of these creatures, doing their own thing
A date or a plate, laws of the jungle reign
Such a strange world, twisting all around
From the sky to the water, dancing on the ground

Iguanas sitting still, soaking in the sun
Jaguars moving smooth, rarely see one
Kangaroos with a spring, hopping to the scene
Loons singing tunes, waking up the dream
Monkeys learning tricks, getting ready for the show
Narwhales knowing depths, a thousand feet will go
Owls calling who, will be meeting their end
Pelicans diving through, gravity is a friend

Chorus

Quails blending in, listen to their song
Ravens steal the light, the jokers never wrong
Snakes find a hole, reap what you sew
Turtles flee the land, the water is their home
Unicorns from a myth, a dream or a tale
Vultures sense a death, hoping that you fail
Wolves give a howl, to the light in the night
Xenarthrans from a past, the sloth for left and right
Yaks in the clouds, hear the thundering sound
Zebras and their stripes, no flies will be found

Chorus

Dogs in Dreams

So many dogs
Some say guardians in hell
Is this the land
To which we fell

I Prefer Wolves

Some people like dogs
I prefer wolves
Finding the source
Forever there is

If I Were Born

If I were born a cheetah, I'd run until I flew
If I were born a wolf, I'd howl at the moon
If I were born a horse, I'd find the fields of green
If I were born a bear, I'd seek a cave to sleep
But I was born a human, it is what it is
Finding out a purpose, dreams are where they're in

In the Colosseum

Watching the jackals, fighting for spoils
The elephants so fat, trapped in the soil
The lions give orders, the dragons stay back
The snakes start to creep, hiding from cats

From out of nowhere it seems, ants on the scene
Cover it all, devoured with glee
Gone again, as quick as they came
What just happened, a defeat to claim

Turning on each other, nothing left to lose
Living or dying, the choices at noon
Escape if you can, it sure won't be pretty
Another show, in the colosseum

Monkeys

The lion waits and crouches
The wolves are in a pack
The bear will rise on haunches
Crocodiles staying wet
No fear of their surroundings
The kings of the land
No bother for the monkey
With a stick in its hand
The last words that were said
Before the end was clear
A cage for a bed
Nothing left to fear
Except for other monkeys
With all new sticks and tricks
Some would add security
Building castles, walls of bricks
Others to move to somewhere new
Escaping for at least a while
But always stuck inside the zoo
Says the raven with a smile

The Ants and the Giant

The ants are lining up thickly
Getting ready for a battle quickly
Of a source of energy waiting
With the numbers easy taking
A hundred to one won't stand a chance
Done it before a thousand times
Over and gone before very long
Onto the next bang of the gong

Who will it be it doesn't really matter
With such numbers a bigger platter
An elephant once tried to challenge the state
Within five minutes dinner was ate
Going on and on for thousands of years
Covered the globe full of ant fears
When nothing left will crawl in the mud
Wait for years to hear the sound of the gun

Of a source that's plump and ready to harvest
Another battle to another conquest
Rising again and scanning the scene
Seeing nothing but broken dreams
A wasteland set, it seems a trick
Beaten to it, an outright theft
Find the perpetrator and teach a lesson
Scour the world and get a confession

After some time found a giant with dimes
Stacked to the sky crying it's mine
Glancing at each other the ants do declare
The appetite for more we understand clear
You must be one of us but bigger and stronger
Not to mention to hibernate longer
Looking around the giant makes a statement
If food you want I'll give you a banquet

No matter how much I'm never quite full

A bit like starving, but all that's left is you
If you all line up and crawl into my mouth
You'll see what I mean and empty my cup
No problems says the ants marching in one by one
After a few years it was finally done
The giant thinking smartly how he tricked them all
The ants leaving eggs for death to call
Who beat who in the battle of taking
The ones in the end that started creating

Throw a Bone

Throw a bone
Make a home
See the wolf
All alone

Versions Unfurled

Some people like dogs
Loyalty is their game
Others prefer cats
Silence for the way
Fish in a tank
Seeing underwater
Birds in a cage
Tricks for a cracker
All of these animals
In our human world
Gentle reminders
Of versions unfurled

Birds

Bird Rhythms

With all of the problems
In the world today
Where can you go
To melt all away

Call it a rhythm
Of a different beat
Hearing the singing
From birds being free

It's not so bad
In a life full of blues
The sea and sky
Are the bluest at noon

Birds and Hedges

I wish I was a bird
To fly away far
Escaping the hedges
A primitive yard

Flying Blind

Hear the message
Hear the rhyme
Nothing more
Flying blind

How Many Birds Can I See

How many birds can I see
In a place and over time
Flying in the air or in a tree
All these birds are on my mind
Call it curiosity
Fly away so far and free
But until then I'm human
How many birds can I see

Laughing Ravens

Going through hell
Nobody can escape
So says the raven
Laughing all the way

Mostly Off the Ground

What happened to dinosaurs
Did they turn into birds
Or remained a few lizards
No longer in herds
Who knows why or the reason
Rarely are standing or still
Moving on throughout the seasons
In a flock or sometimes alone
Either way, they go their way
Mostly off the ground
Nest in trees, fly by day
Singing is their sound

Not So, Says the Raven

History repeats itself
So says the broken clock
Not so says the raven
Only stories are bought

Raven Brain

An interesting thing
About ravens they say
The brain is much more
When lighter the weight

Raven in the Band

I once met a raven, on a sunny afternoon
Was at the cliffs on the shore, playing a brand new tune
Landing a few feet from me, and looked me in the eye
At the end of every line I spoke, caws were its reply

After a few more songs were played, cawing for every one
Made my day with a band of strays, the tunes that we sung
How could I give my thanks, what could I do
I searched around in my bag, a few peanuts I threw

It didn't take long for others to see, a trough being opened up
The seagulls landing everywhere, they'll take it all in one gulp
The raven picked up its stash, and said I'm out of here
The ones in flocks are not my stock, I laugh at all their fears

As the times went by I tried again, but it never did work out
Only gulls surrounded me, all they did was cry and shout
What happened to that raven, flying off to a foreign land
I'll never forget that afternoon, with a raven in the band

Ravens at Play

Soaring up and down
By the cliffs on the shore
A never ending current
Opened up are doors

Circling higher and higher
Rising from the stream
Cruising by the edges
Diving towards the sea

In and out of the fray
Throughout the afternoon
Nothing to fear, time for play
Knowing it's over, much too soon

Ship of Jays

Seeing the joker, walking up a path
Crossing a snake, all shiny and black
Going a bit further, to the top of the hill
Take a look around, at the barren field
Where can you go, who can you find
Where can you reach, in the land of the blind
Two ships flying high, merging in the sky
Hearing the songs, never knowing why

Chorus
Feeling the sun, dancing in the rain
Hopping on board, the ship of jays
Floating on through, the doorway of dreams
Falling brand new, in the diamond sea

Seeing the puppet, walking without strings
Into the air, swimming in streams
Trained from birth, doing what he's told
Struggled so hard, breaking the mold
Cutting with a knife, burning with a flame
Waiting for the night, tricks of the trade
Run through the trees, connecting to free
Finally resting, in the cool morning breeze

Chorus

Seeing the king, of his own mind
Never had wealth, but could read all the signs
Exiled from his kingdom, starting over again
Begin at the bottom, find a new friend
Fighting off the dragons, the fate that was given
Alone at a cave, the end of a mission
On the edge of a mountain, gazing at the stars
Falling asleep, until the morning calls

Chorus

Watching Out For Glimpses

Born in a hidden cave
Near the water on the cliffs
Hear the crashing waves
Feel the foggy mist

The full moon brings a look
Curious to explore
Peeking out for a bit
A hundred feet the shore

Stretching out for a leap
Stepping off the ledge
Soaring on the breeze
Rising drafts there is

Higher and farther
Through clouds to the stars
Moving from the water
Where the cities are

Spotting all the dots
From cars, trucks and trains
Lines getting bright
Drawing to the stage

Staying up and high
No need for such attention
Skyscrapers in the night
Perches for relaxing

Watching all the people
Running in the streets
Sirens to the steeple
Searching for the thief

Minutes turn to hours
Ra is rising soon
Opening are the flowers
Catch the morning dew

Returning to the cave
Another night has passed
The same as ancient days
Forever seems to last

Why or what's the purpose
Biding time to know
Watching out for glimpses
Of curses letting go

When Seagulls Squall

When seagulls squall
A fish is doomed
The pelicans follow
Ghosts of the loon

The Sun

Drying Up

Feel the sun
Next to the fire
Dry up the rain
The smoke rising higher

Energy

Energy everywhere
Like dots in the night
Some are connecting
Others in flight

Feel the Sun Shining

I feel the sun, reaching down to the core
Melting the ice, from the winter before
What's after that, sparkling on the waves
Even trying to count, will drive you insane
If you look too closely, in moments you're blind
Sitting on the edge, of a steeper incline
Enjoy it while you can, soon enough will be dark
Only in your dreams, can you find the spark

Chorus
Feel the sun shining, so warm and bright
From dawn to dusk, Ra wins the fight
Everything you see, shadows from the source
The air you breathe, the stories of old

It has so many fights, all along the way
The fog and clouds, will darken the day
The seasons have their trends, nothing can be done
An eclipse at noon, a Hail Mary has won
Our work in a building, at home indoors
Watching the tube, a repetitive bore
Playing a game, laying on the couch
It's all the same, the sun is left out

Chorus

With so many stars, shining in the night
Only the closest, will give you sight
From myths long ago, to the science of today
No energy so great, as the dawn of the day
Getting to the end, sinking to the depths
The sun is lost, a light has wept
Scorching the earth, become a wasteland
Rise from the ashes, in a foreign land

Chorus

Fly to the Sun

Give me the sun
Let me burn to a crisp
Higher and higher
Up through the mist

Where it will end
I really don't care
It's been cold so long
Froze in the lair

Not any longer
Hear the morning roar
Break off the yoke
Fly through the air

Goodnight to the Sun

As Ra starts to fade
Into the oceans of blue
A calm on display
The end coming soon

A season of winter
If only the night
Now and forever
Time taking flight

The buildings blending
In the shadow of trees
Space is trending
To only what's near

One last burst
Before it's all done
The wind blowing crisp
Goodnight to the sun

More the Merrier

Some say it can be blinding
Looking too close when shining
Seeing the colors, merging together
Strands reaching, seeming forever
Except the plants, no worries for them
Staring all day, straight in the sun
A race to the top, gather the yellow
Adding some blue from rainy weather
Remains that are seen, ending in green
Stretching for more, branches to leaves

Ode to the Sun

When it's cold and windy, clouds fill the sky
Pulling up your jacket, in the warmth you hide
When all of a sudden, out of nowhere
The sun comes shining, no more despair

Chorus
I feel the sun, shining on me
I feel the sun, just like a tree
I feel the sun, all is ok
I feel the sun, smiles for play

With a little rain, everything will bloom
Smells and colors, fill up the room
Spring has arrived, that time again
Friends to gather, wounds to mend

Chorus

Sitting by the water, an ocean or lake
Millions of sparkles, a diamond bay
Hearing the waves, singing in its praise
Into the air, the water will raise

Chorus

Ra is Winning

The wind is blowing
Ravens are spinning
Waves are crashing
Ra is winning

Sky Watching

As the sun starts to rise
The sky turns to blue
A cloud or a wave
A change coming soon

Getting near the peak
A brightened white and yellow
The winds no longer meek
Raging with a bellow

Feeling for the loss
The stories all but written
No matter what the cost
Energy is venting

As the sun starts to set
The sky turns to red
Next turning black
Stars a point to head

The Rise and Set

Rise in the east
Set in the west
What's in between
Out of the nest

Seasons and Weather

A Cycle Brings

Earth to fire
Water to air
Moving faster
When all is clear

Drop the weight
In early spring
Settle down
A cycle brings

Where it goes
Nobody knows
How long it lasts
The present shows

After a Storm

Seeing the sun
Break out of the storm
No longer a question
Of the new norm
Feeling the sun
After a storm
Is there anything better
When tired and worn

Cycles

The mountains and rivers of ancient lore
Descending to deserts, vultures galore
Approaching the sea, horizons of dreams
Catching the boat, that floats on the breeze

Living in Spring

Some people see
The surface of things
A tree growing roots
Living in spring

Morning Rain

Hear the rain falling, the splashing of the puddles
Nobody heading out today, without their black umbrellas
In the early morning setting, before the sun is rising
The trees are set for blowing, down their seeds are falling
The ocean over yonder, the waves crashing harder
The rain has returned, time making stronger
Every drop that's hitting, I feel my eyes closing
Going back to bed, for a much longer dozing

Scenes

Clouds and dreams
Shaping the scene
Right as rain
Left to clean

Seasons of Change

With leaves of color in the autumn breeze
Float to the ground before the freeze
Birds flying high fill up the sky
To a warmer place in southern climes
Halloween with masks for a mockery
Light a fire to help the spirits free
Harvest time in what we call fall
The seasons change for one and all

The flurries fall and cover up the ground
The lakes to freeze hear the crackling sound
The wolves to howl at the midnight moon
The owls in the night calling who
Burn up a log make a pot of chili
Count the stars can see so many
It's winter time until the next thaw
The seasons change for one and all

Feel the sun begin to break on through
Melting away for something new
The seeds to bloom filling up the fields
The fish are jumping no ice to yield
The birds are back building their nests
The roads are clear for a farther trek
Spring has arrived a bouncing ball
The seasons change for one and all

The temperature rising and a longer day
So much to do, some work and play
The crops are growing, the lakes are full
The music playing, the stories are told
Flying by see the time go quick
Over too soon, feeling like a trick
The summers gone, shadows growing tall
The seasons change for one and all

Spring Thaw

The ice finally melted
What took so long this year
The north taking over
The summer sheds a tear
How long will it last
What will change the trend
Back to seasons past
Another cycle to amend

The Dripping Rain

The rain keeps falling three days straight
Long overdue from the year long fate
Sometimes harder and coming down as waves
Others lighter a mist in the morning haze
Either way the drops never stop
Over and over fill the cup
Hard to stay awake in days of the rain
Hypnotic nature to settle your brain
Getting reset, a recharge for days ahead
Until then it's recovery and resting in bed
From going too hard or too much
Feeling to fly without any crutch
No sleep needed and walking miles in cold
With a dozen drinks to fuel and embold
Days go by getting higher and farther
Then the crash and onto recover
All better now getting ready for another
Windmills everywhere giants discovered
Not today for the time isn't ready
The rain says only for the slow and steady
In the meantime order is the tune that is played
With the beats ever pounding, the dripping rain

The Upcoming Storm

Getting excited for the upcoming storm
Too much humidity, beyond any norm
Flashes of lightning, hearing the thunder
Seeing the darkened, clouds ever closer
The wind picking up, trees blowing sideways
Down comes the rain, stayed for the day
And into the night, the battle rages on
Staying inside, hearing the song
Until the dawn, when all has been settled
Starting anew, leaving the shelter
Hearing the birds, sound the all clear
Stepping outside, feeling the cheer